I0437039

How To Be A Full Time Writer

Through Ghostwriting, Freelance Writing, Editing, Co-Writing and Your Writing

Kristen James

How To Be A Full Time Writer and Editor

Through Ghostwriting, Freelance Writing, Editing, Co-Writing and Your Writing

ISBN 978-1475284959

Also by Kristen James:
Book Promoting 101: How To Tell The World About Your Book
How To Sell More Kindle eBooks

A Cowboy For Christmas
More Than Memories
The Enemy's Son
The Fairy and her Giant
The River People

View Amazon Author Profile and Book List at
http://amazon.com/author/kristenjames

Learn more at
www.writerkristenjames.com
www.facebook.com/WriterKristenJames
Twitter: @writerkristenj

Contents

Let's Have Some Fun

Do you enjoy your job? You should! If you don't, I'd love to help you create a job you love. I'm having fun writing this ebook and hope you enjoy reading it. I'll share everything I know on this topic, and you can choose which steps and tips will benefit you.

My life motto is: life should be an adventure. Sure, there are things beyond our control, but there are so many things we can change. These days, we can choose our job and hours, or even create our job through a vast array of online resources. So, would you like to work part or full time from home, earning a living through something you love? This 70 page guide will show you how I've done it, and how you can start freelancing right now.

I began editing and publishing, as a hobby, in 2006 and ran a short story journal for about a year before I stepped into book publishing. It grew from there, and since 2008, I've been working as a publisher and ghostwriter using freelancing sites and my publishing website. Throughout that time, more and more of my work showed up in my email without me searching for it.

Now that I'm moving toward working solely on my own books, I want to share what I've learned with you. Most of this information will lean toward full time ghostwriting and freelance writing, and near the end, I'll also look at how to grow your income with your own books like I'm doing.

Here's to your adventure as a writer!

Full Time Pay, Not Full Time Work

I write all the time because I love to write. I've always worked on several "work" projects and at least one of my own. If I weren't a novelist and worked only on freelance projects, I would probably spend much less time writing.

If you're writing as a freelancer to support yourself, you might not want to put in 6, 8, or 10 hour days, or work five days a week.

So "full time" in this book means making a full time living, defined by how much money you need to make. Some people want more freedom and are happy living on two thousand a month or even less. Other people are after the big book projects and want to earn four, five or six thousand a month. Your goal might be to make a full time salary on four or five hours a day, and that's the point of being self employed.

It's possible to start off at the pay level you want or need, and it can also take a little time to build up to it. Once you gain some experience, you can earn more per project, per page, so that you don't have to work as much.

I love what I do because my work is my passion, and then I can take a few hours or even the day off when I need to or want to do something else. As long as you're responsible about finishing projects on time, I think it's fine to set your schedule the way you want it. This book is about creating a job you love that allows you to allocate your time the way you want. Let's get started!

What Does it Take?

Over the last year or so, there have been many blogs and articles written about independent author success stories. There are books and blogs about how to make a living selling your novels as ebooks. It's rewarding and fun to be an author, but it usually takes a few years to gain a readership and make money at it. However, you don't need to be a bestselling author, or even a full time author, to be a full time writer earning several thousand a month or more.

There are plenty of writers finding all kinds of writing work through freelance sites and their own website. Realistically, you can use the tips in this book to help you be a full time freelancer with web design, photography and art. I just will speak from my experience with writing, editing and publishing.

I will show you all the steps I took to become a full time writer, working from home. You might be a creative writer like me and enjoy writing short stories and novels, or you might be purely technical and want to write product descriptions and college papers. You might even be a mix of creative and technical or have a different niche. Luckily there's a surprising demand for all formats of writing and writing related work including:

- grant writing
- articles
- web content
- research papers
- ebooks
- books
- personal projects
- fiction
- critiquing
- editing and more.

I've ghostwritten business books, "How To" and description articles and ebooks, Utube dialogue, cast of characters, family stories, wedding speeches, novels and memoirs.

So what does it take? Just a few things, actually:

A Computer and Internet Connection
Skill
Discipline
A small investment – you can join freelancing sites for free but the paid memberships get much better results.

It's very easy to come by a computer and internet, but the second two might stop some from trying.

How much skill does it take? You need to be able to write clearly and correctly, of course. This means education and/or extensive experience. Degrees look nice on your freelancer profile, but your work samples really show your expertise. If you're starting out and wanting to create a career in writing (at least for a while) you can learn to write well through reading, a few courses and practice.

I personally think "Discipline" will stop more people than the skill aspect. If you're worried about this being a roadblock, just remember you're working for pay. The money is usually at the end of the project, at least when you're starting out. (I'll talk more about milestones and down payments soon.)

It does take discipline to be your own boss, but the rewards are huge. They include:

- Setting your own hours.
- Saving time and money without a commute.

- The satisfaction of working for yourself and doing something you love – this one is huge!
- Control over your income instead of having someone else decide your fixed salary and vacation time.
- The ability to bid more and bid higher to give yourself a raise.
- The ability to expand or change your services to adjust to the economy and market.
- You can be home if you need to – no calling in sick or scrambling to find a babysitter for your sick kids.
- Freedom to arrange your workday as you like.
- Tax credits and breaks for business purchases and office space in your home.
- Choosing your focus and projects. (The more experience you gain, the more choices you have. We'll talk about a work portfolio and reviews soon too.)

When you're self employed, there's no boss to give the promotion to someone else. It's all about you and your ability.

Of course there's different levels of commitment. Some of you might be starting a writing business while others want to supplement their income. You can do this as a job, a part time job, a hobby or a way to earn a little extra cash here and there. I worked as a freelance writer to earn a living while I got my fiction writing career off the ground.

My Story

Mrs. Straight, my fourth grade teacher, introduced me to the short story. She liked my creation so much that she asked me to read it at an assembly with parents, teachers and students. Before long, I had handwritten my first "novel" in a notebook called *Wilderness Love*. I saved my allowance and bought a typewriter. After typing several novels on that, my family bought a computer, which conveniently went into my bedroom. By the ninth grade, I had subscribed to Writer's Digest and was submitting my novels to publishers. It would be a while before I saw any results, but that's part of the publishing game. After high school, I went to my local community college and took all their creative writing classes before graduating in 1999.

I continued writing and submitting to publishers, and in 2005, I received my first request letter from a publisher to see more of a romance novel. This was a first step of many. I got several rejections on full manuscripts from the big publishing houses and then was finally accepted by two smaller presses starting in 2006. I took a year of creative writing classes at Southern Oregon University that year, and had a short story published by Skive Quarterly out of Australia. It was my first published piece since it came out before the novels.

It was about that time that I found www.lulu.com, a print on demand publisher that allows writers to upload and publisher their own books. Even though I was getting published traditionally, I wanted to explore other options as well. (I was surprised at how very long it took to go through the publishing process with a traditional publisher. They waited a year to even start editing. That process took quite a while, and then they waited a year after that to publish the book.) So, I self published *The River People*.

I've always enjoyed art and design, so I liked putting the cover and interior design together to create a print book. I enjoyed the process so much, I launched a quarterly short story journal. I began light editing for others. Within a year, I was also accepting books and calling my little enterprise Brilliant Book Press.

In 2008, I changed my online publishing company into a self publishing company called Bravado Publishing. All this really took was creating a professional website with lots of information. This allowed me to open the doors to many more authors than I could publish under a traditional model, and it also allowed me to begin to make a living with my passion. A growing number of people across the US hired me to help with editing and/or publishing, and I began working with several different local authors on color children's books. I had one author publish four books with me, several authors published three, and several more published two books from 2008 to 2011.

After stepping into self publishing in 2008, and then finding editing work through my website, I began to wonder, how else can I make money from home? I knew there would be sites where I could find more editing work. I searched and found www.ifreelance.com, where I could bid for freelance writing and editing.

Along with bidding through iFreelance, I added a page to my Bravado Publishing website about ghostwriting and editing.

My first ghostwriting project was writing outdoor articles. Another early job was an ebook about growing and caring for roses. Along with articles, ebooks, website content and editing, and some 'spinning' jobs where the buyer had a bunch of articles and wanted them rewritten. I'll warn you now, these rewriting or spinning jobs are the most mind-numbing ones and usually have horrible pay. The buyers seem to think they're quick and easy, but my creative mind would rather write new material and rework someone else's. I don't recommend these jobs.

I searched and bid on all kinds of creative writing and book length projects. The first book project I won was a business book on patents. I didn't know a thing about patents, but somehow the buyer and I clicked. He liked my writing style and supplied his published articles and internal business memos. I used these along with his outline and guidance to write the book. I ended up working with him on several books, a few journal papers, editing and other odds and ends related to writing.

All of the freelancing sites have creative writing projects, book projects, and all kinds of other writing. You should look for the kind of work you enjoy, whether it's articles, product descriptions, sales copy, grant writing or speeches.

I eventually joined more freelancing sites and then gravitated toward one, but iFreelance is a good starter site. Looking back, there seemed to be more of the small, lower paying jobs that I could get as a beginner.

It's good to have more than one site for finding jobs, and you may want to start on one and quickly add another. After gaining some experience and getting used to working as a freelancer, I added www.elance.com next and really liked it. I searched for jobs on both sites and noticed some were posted on both. This means it's not awarded on one of the sites, and some jobs are never awarded. So you do end up bidding quite a bit. On the brighter side, I did find more jobs because many jobs were only on one site.

After that I found www.guru.com and created a profile there as well. However, I found Guru to be more competitive so I had a profile there for about a year while working on the first two sites. Once I began using Guru more, it still took a few months to win projects. It really helped once I was able to show work experience and samples from the other sites.

I also worked through a site called Demand Studios, www.demandstudios.com, which allows you to claim articles titles that interest you, write them and submit them for review. If accepted by their freelance editors (and yes, you can apply to do that as well) the article goes live online at sites like Ehelp or Happy News. Sometimes they have you do some edits. The pay, when I used the site, was $15 for a short, 500 word article, with your byline. They added some shorter and some longer lengths with other pay levels while I was using the site. They're always adding new things, so I'm sure they offer even more options now. When I joined the site, it only took a short application and a writing sample.

Demand Studios is very helpful in several ways. The first is there are thousands of topics to search and choose from, so you can write about things that interest you. The articles require cited sources, so you can even learn about new things. Finally, the different article formats all have templates where you fill in each section. You get to start with the title they give you and a format, so these are fairly easy to write.

Working through four different sites allowed me to search for things I wanted to write about. Sometimes I found interesting things on most of the sites, and other times it seemed all my work came from one.

Once I had several years of experience, I began to move more and more on Guru. It's the biggest site and had the most jobs, plus it also had an escrow account to protect buyers and freelancers.

For me, it's exciting and fun to have different projects. Every publishing project taught me something new about formatting. Each writing project taught me something about writing or a new subject, or something new on a familiar subject.

Another fun aspect of freelancing is meeting all kinds of people and developing working relationships. I had client from the United Arab Emirates that hired me to write a business book about engaging employees. I would work on it during the day, send it to him, and then get up in the morning to find his email with comments, additional information and feedback. With this around the work schedule, we wrote this book in a month. He hired me for several books and paid four to six thousand, and with the short timeframe, these were my highest paying jobs for the time. I've done quite a bit of other work for him as well, including Powerpoint presentations, brochures and editing.

Another fun client was a woman who had me co-write an ebook about the dangers of texting and driving. I helped on several more ebooks for kids, some website content and even the written content for an iphone app.

There's a surprising variety of writing needs out there. Several times, I've been hired to write plots for Utube skits, or a cast of characters. I've written about ice fishing, caring for decks, potty training pets, parenting, women's issues, wedding speeches, books on proposing, relationships and a lot of "How To."

Some of the easiest jobs for me are nonfiction articles or ebooks that offer instructions or advice. These projects are easy to define in terms of pages and content. (I'll talk about writing a project agreement soon.) There are a ton of them out there, too. Editing is the other plentiful type of work, but there are also many freelance editors competing for these jobs. If you enjoy editing and can show talent and expertise, you can win these. I bid on some editing work but enjoy writing, and I feel that's more my expertise.

Are you excited yet? Let's talk about the nuts and bolts.

Getting Started: Ghostwriting and Freelancing

You can start online freelancing and have a project within a week. Maybe sooner.

Step 1: Gather all your work samples

Since you're reading this book, I'm going to guess that you have all kinds of writing on your computer such as college papers, short stories, novel(s), articles, resumes, letters and more. Maybe you've done some freelance work already.

Pick the ten best pieces of writing you have. I'd suggest making a copy of the file and putting into a new folder called Writing Samples. (I create a folder for every job to hold the work agreement, any note files, attachments the employer sends, your research and the actual project file. Label everything clearly!) Your writing samples will go into your online work portfolio on each freelancing site you use. They will also help you see if you have a niche or focus.

When you first begin bidding on jobs, it just looks better to already have some writing, or "work" samples so prospective clients can see your writing style. You can add to these and switch them out later on too.

Even with writing and work samples in your portfolio, you will win many more jobs if you attach a file to your bid. It can even be from your portfolio, but it makes it easier for the employer to look at it. I've seen comments in project descriptions that said freelancers who didn't send attachments would not be considered.

So while the work portfolio is very important, it's just as important to attach a relevant writing sample to each bid.

No Work Samples?

I can see how some technical writers might not have relevant work samples for an online portfolio. Let's say you're planning to write instruction manuals, product descriptions or other technical projects, but you haven't written any yet.

You can create writing samples for your portfolio by writing a few short articles, sales pages or a "sample" page so it looks like it's from a bigger project.

Think of one of your hobbies or something you can do such as building a bird house. Then write a step by step guide on how to do it. If you need to learn how to write these, spend some time on eHow and look at the format of highly rated articles.

Look up some sales pages online or ads for any kind of product you like or use. Then write a one page sales ad or website content.

I've even created short samples for a project I want to bid on. If I wanted to bid on a project but didn't have any samples from another paid project, I would write a paragraph or two that showed that type of writing, and include this either as an attachment or pasted at the end of my bid. It's enough to show you can handle the material, but not enough that you wasted your time if you don't get that job.

Step 2: Join site(s) and create a profile

I'd recommend starting on one site, at least for a few weeks so you don't overwhelm yourself. (Go ahead and check into sites like Demand Studios that are free to join.) The exception to this is if you just lost your job, or underwent some other circumstance, and need to make a full income in a hurry.

The other reason you may want to start on one site is there is a membership fee. Every site I've used had free memberships and different levels of paying memberships. I started on the free memberships to look around and see if I liked the site. It didn't take long for me to learn that it's much harder to win jobs with a free membership. The paid ones are worth the investment simply because you get placed higher in the list of bids, and you're marked as a paying member. It looks more professional.

I've sometimes bought the 6 month or year membership options, and other times I've paid monthly. There were times when I had so much work I let my paid membership expire and turn into a nonpaying profile. When I went back and bid with a free membership, I didn't get work. So when I wanted to win jobs again, I always upgraded.

Most sites let you withdraw all or part of your balance, so you can leave some of your pay behind to use for membership fees.

I'll talk more about your profile first and then cover bidding.

Freelancer Profile

Your freelancer identity, at first glance, is made up of your screen name and a picture. This is your first chance to look professional.

I see quite a few that use something like "Mjay999" or something you might see on Twitter. These kinds of screen names don't seem to win nearly as many jobs.

I currently use "Kristen James, Bestselling Author" for my screen name. This is because I've focused more and more on creative writing.

Before this one, I used, "Kristen James, Author and Publisher" and even just "Bravado Publishing and Writing" because there were many jobs that wanted expertise in writing, formatting and publishing.

You can highlight your niche here too, such as:

Susan Smith, Grant Writer

or Pam Potter, Copywriting that sells!

I've noticed odd names like "Mjay999" are often coupled with a random snapshot that should be on Facebook and not a professional freelancing sight. Would that make you want to hire someone?

It doesn't take much to take a professional headshot. It shows up in a one inch box so you don't need to go fork out a bunch of money for it either. Really. But you should have on a nice shirt and look professional.

After these two items, you'll create a description of your services.

It's true that you don't want to limit yourself, but it's also true that people like to hire an expert for what they need. So if you have a lot of experience or know how in a certain area, go ahead and highlight this. You don't have to list every type of writing known to man.

My Guru profile shows most of my earnings through ghostwriting and books. That gives me expert power when I bid on a book project.

I've used long descriptions that talked about different types of writing in the past. Because I've focused more and more on creative fiction projects, I focused my description to that and have a short description now.

This is my actual description on Guru.com:

"I'm a full time author and enjoy working on freelance projects to help others experience the joy of seeing their idea in book form. My writing is making its way onto the big screen even. My published work includes A Cowboy For Christmas (Kindle bestseller), The River People (#1 category bestseller), More Than Memories, Embers of Hope, A Miraculous Fate and Kauai Spy Games. You can read more about my novels at www.writerkristenjames.com."

I probably can't win any grant writing or technical projects with this, but I usually win the projects I want.

The more you write your description to your skill set and passions, the more jobs you'll win.

Notes:

Do you need a Website?

The popular advice out there for novelists, freelancers and even entrepreneurs is, yes, of course every new business needs a website.

However, this isn't a one size fits all question and answer. If you're launching a full service writing and editing business, a website is a good idea. You can feature different services on different pages and supply short examples.

You can offer the services I discuss in this book:
Ghostwriting
Business Writing
Web Content
Articles
Critiquing
Editing
Proof Reading

And you can include other services such as:
Cover Design (if you have graphic and design experience.)
Interior Formatting for ebooks and/or print
Publishing (but most people want to publish themselves these days, so I would make this an expanded service that offers people assistance in publishing their work themselves.)

A website can also help you look more professional to potential clients on freelancing sites, where your link is displayed.

I had a website for Bravado Publishing until recently. It evolved over time as my services did. At first it highlighted my print on demand publishing offerings and editing. It grew to showcase my ghostwriting, outdoor writing, critiquing and ebook and print formatting.

Your own website is an additional cost of $10 to $30 per month for web hosting. It's worth it for a business, and possibly for a writer who wants to showcase many different types of writing and services. It also helps you show more of your personality and passion.

If spending a little more for website isn't an issue, you can use it to draw in more work, and attract clients who might not join a freelancing site as a buyer. These people might find you online by searching for their specific need, so it will draw more people in if you list your niche services and qualifications.

All that said, I've seen freelancers with high earnings who have just the profile on the freelance site. As a fiction writer, I get much more traffic and interaction on my Facebook author page. I'm not sure I'd recommend a professional freelancer using Facebook as their main website, but it's a good option for adding another point of contact. Facebook pages come up high in internet searches, which is one more positive thing about it. Plus they're free.

Really, you can get started with freelancer profiles on different freelance sites, since these are included with your membership fees. Then you can build from there or see if using just the freelancer profile draws in enough work by itself.

Step 3: Bidding

Once you have your screen name, photo and work samples uploaded, it's time to bid.

You can look at all the writing jobs and then sort them by budget, most recently posted or other factors. I do this and then I search using keywords based on my interests.

I've won many jobs that I found by searching about fishing, but not just a generic "fishing" search term. I searched for steelhead, salmon and Oregon. One of these jobs was editing the quarterly issues of Kype Magazine, which I still do.

I also search for parenting, tween, cycling, camping, outdoors, hiking and berries. You probably have a completely different set of interests, but you get the idea. You can use knowledge and passion you already have for freelancing jobs. This passion comes across in your bid and helps you win projects. Plus, as you develop a work history in a certain area, you'll be the obvious choice for any related project.

When I'm looking for work, I search for projects I'm qualified to do, and then I decide if the project interests me. I've also developed a list of red flags that will send me running away from a project. I'll cover these soon in a separate section. If I see one of my red flags, or have a bad feeling of any kind about the project description, I don't bid.

Sometimes a client will award a project to you based solely on your bid. Other times they'll email and discuss the project with you. Again, there are a few red flags to watch for at this point. If you don't like how things are going, it's fine to walk away.

Once the client feels satisfied that you're the right person, they'll award the job. Every site allows you to accept or decline a project award.

At this point, you should create a project agreement that includes the description (pulled from the site, written by the client), your bid, the agreed upon fee and pay points, the timeline, and any other items to clarify the project.

Many sites will have you upload this agreement so the client can review and accept it, or request changes.

Most sites tell you to wait for the down payment or money put into escrow before you begin work. I've always required either a down payment or escrow when I work with someone for the first time. Most clients are fine with putting money into escrow.

After you begin, it's a good idea to send material early on. Edit and polish it, make it your best, but send the first five or so pages. Every once in a while, a client will say, "Whoa! This isn't what I envisioned." Then you can discuss and adjust the project. This starts a good communication flow and keeps the project on track. You don't want to write 20 or 30 pages to discover you had a different idea than your client.

Meet all your agreed upon deadlines.

It's good to include a point in the project agreement about how many edits you will perform. For the most part, clients have asked me to change a few things or simply accepted the work. There were times, however, when someone wanted me to edit, and edit, and edit... This is usually about the client and not you. These kinds of clients will do this and then demand that you cut your fee or drop the last pay point. I'll explain more of these later, under "Red Flags."

If you communicate and send work for feedback, you should be able to move the project along to completion.

After a final review, the client will release the escrow or pay the final invoice.

Then it's time to get a review. Some sites, such as Guru, will send the client an email asking them to leave you a review, and that helps to get them.

So, just how involved should a client be in a project? You can sometimes tell from the project description if they'd like to supply the outline, notes and some writing. Other times you'll gather this from talking to them. I've had some very involved clients and other who told me the title and outline, or just their idea, and let me go with it.

Bid Format:

Introduction: (The first two items can be switched around.)

A sentence or two about who you are, usually as a writer, and it's even better if you can relate this to the project's topic or format.

What drew you in or interested you. Tell them why the project sounds exciting, intriguing or a good match for you. These first two items can show that you read the description and understand what the client needs.

The main part – your qualifications. Wow the client with your experience that is related to this project.

You can include some personal (but not overly personal!) and friendly information that might relate to the project or client in some way.

Closing:
Thanks for your consideration…
Thank you for considering me…
I look forward to discussing the project more… (I personally don't like this one too much. Sometimes it sounds a bit pushy when people write it to me.)

Your name and links

To illustrate these, I'll share some of my winning bids.

Sample Winning Bids

These are some of my winning bids for projects in the $300 to $800 range.

Project: Critique a Middle Grade Novel

My Bid:

I'm intrigued by your plot and would enjoy critiquing and editing your novel. I'm a published author (both traditionally and self published) and I run a self publishing services company. One of my novels, The River People, targets young adults to teens, and I've critiqued and edited many middle grade novels. I make small edits with tracking and insert notes on the plot, characters, story movement, age level, flow, dialogue, and anything that will improve the book.

I estimate about a month or less for this job to allow time for you to review it as we move through the book.

I recently critiqued and edited a middle grade novel for a local writer who was also a school teacher. His book featured a young boy who loved to fish who was facing several life changes.

My bid includes a PDF copy of *Book Promoting 101: How To Tell The World About Your Book*, which received 5 stars from Midwest Book Review. After you finish the writing phase, I also offer formatting, converting and publishing services.

Thanks so much for considering me,
Kristen James

Project: ghostwriting ebooks on parenting

My Bid:

I would love to write two ebooks on parenting for you. I'm a bestselling Kindle author with extensive experience ghostwriting everything from self help, to business to fiction. I've also written quite a few articles targeting women that were epublished under my name.

Parenting is a topic close to my heart. I have three children ages 8, 10 and 11, and also three stepchildren ages 9, 12 and 16. I'm learning so much from raising all these kids, and now I sometimes watch moms with toddlers and wish I could offer some pointers. But that's not something you do unless you know them well! Writing ebooks on the topic would be a nice outlet. That's why I bid on this project; I look for ebooks or books that really interest me.

Along with your guidance on the topics, layout and structure, I can use my own knowledge and research to write these ebooks, plus any input or outline you have.

I'm a quick writer and would love to get started on this project!

Thanks for considering me,
Kristen James

***

As you gain experience, you'll get invited to bid on projects. This gives you a foot in the door, unless the client invited 250 freelancers. I see this here and there, but most of the time, I'm invited with a few other freelancers or just by myself.

The follow is a bid I wrote for a project where the client invited only me, and then awarded the job right away.

***

Project: Editing and Layout for Business Book

My Bid:

Hello and thank you for inviting me to bid on your editing/layout project. I've ghostwritten and edited numerous business books, and would be happy to polish yours. I also format books on a regular basis through my publishing company. It sounds like you plan to publish to print?

A fee of $250 may cover this project if it's a shorter book. I'd be happy to look over the file and confirm that or make a final bid.

I look forward to your reply,
Kristen James
(list of my websites.)
(I also attached samples of books that I edited and formatted.)

This was a winning bid for a full length book project with a budget of $5000 – $10,000. The project description asked for the bidder's writing history and education.

I'm a published author and ghostwriter with experience in writing action, spy, mystical, romance, Native American fiction and general fiction. I've co-written an action/spy thriller titled *Kauai Spy Games* with Jeff Ivanov and a mystical thriller titled *A Miraculous Fate* with Tommy Garrison.

I take on one book project at a time and currently have an opening for a large project like this. My turnaround time is 3-5 months, depending upon the book's length and the response time from the buyer.

I began writing in grade school and studied creative writing through high school and college at Umpqua Community College and Southern Oregon University. I found many valuable classes and coupled these with extensive outside study and practice. I wrote many novels before my published ones, which you can review at www.writerkristenjames.com. The site contains some of my professional and reader reviews, teasers and excerpts from my novels, and a few short stories. I write my novels in scenes just as a movie is constructed, and this also means I write tight, fast paced plots without the parts readers skip.

Thanks so much for considering me,
Kristen James
www.writerkristenjames.com
www.bookpromoting101.com - a blog and a book. Midwest Book Review gave rated the book 5 stars.

Bidding Tips:

Do not say you just started. (You have ten work samples and you'll attach something relevant to your bid.)

Proofread your bid! Imagine an employer sending you a message to point out a typo. I write my bid in Word and then paste it into the bid form. This allows me to enlarge the text, and although you shouldn't rely solely on Word's proofreader, it does help.

Related to this, make sure your freelance profile is error free and uses correct grammar. Ditto on a website, if you use one.

Keep up on the projects and bid early. You can do this by logging in once a day and checking the new project postings, and by have the site send you an email of new project matches. (Most sites do this automatically or have you set up your preferences when you join.) I've had quite a few clients tell me they awarded the job to me because I bid early on and wrote a detailed, targeted bid. They could tell I carefully read the project description and tailored my bid to it.

This might sound a bit obvious, but it's important. Most of these sites let you save bids as a template for future use. The problem here is, then your bids will sound generic unless you rework them. I've saved quite a few templates, and then found I always completely rework them.

Most sites will send you an email of new project matches. I still get them every day from Guru.

You'll win more jobs if:

You're bid is detailed and longer than a paragraph. Customize it, even if you start with a template.

You show that you understand the project and have worked on similar ones.

You're upbeat and positive.

You don't point out what others will do wrong or what other freelancers are missing. Focus on the value you bring.

You highlight your strengths. This is done through showing successful jobs.

You show how you'll benefit the project, both through your writing expertise and experience, and your real world experience and passions.

You use concrete examples. I've seen a few bids or comments that said, "I've ghostwrote a ton of books." Anyone can say that.

Forget your fears and worries. If you see a big book project (or whatever type of project you're after) and you feel you can't win it, bid anyway. I won some big projects early on by writing a terrific, positive bid that included several strong work samples. Sometimes, it comes down to the writer's style. The client wants to connect and click with a writer or editor on a personal level. They'll look for someone with a style they like. So you might win a high paying project with your voice, style and personality.

On the flip side, you won't get projects that you're perfectly qualified for because someone else had the right style or fit. Don't worry about it, and especially don't let it get you down. Just keep going and keep bidding.

Remember you'll win more and more projects as you gain experience. These sites list your reviews and previous earnings, and clients tend to hire people with a positive work history. Some of the freelancing sites will tell you what percentage of projects you're winning. For the first year, I won about 10% of the projects I bid on. I've read this is an excellent return for direct mail ads! It also gives you an idea of how many projects you need to bid on to win enough.

A General Tip:

The user agreement on most freelancing sites states that you agree to keep all payment through the given site. That means freelancers shouldn't find a job on the site and then arrange for payment through a different method that cuts out the site. You might run into a buyer that wants to pay you through check, Paypal, or other money transfer method, and you might wonder why that's bad. For one, the site makes this kind of work possible. For another, it's very bad for you. All of your earnings show up on your freelancer profile. It makes you look like a desirable freelancer if your earnings are higher. You'll have more reviews for more projects too. If you don't have those earnings and reviews, it's harder to get future jobs.

This is also a good reason to focus on one freelancing site, or perhaps try for a high level of work across two or three. The people with high earnings and reviews look like they write full time, and they get more projects.

Pricing

Bidding online can be competitive. At first, you can win projects by bidding lower than more experienced writers. Guru, however, does not show everyone's bid amount. Some sites give the buyer (client) the option to show everyone's bids or to keep these confidential.

Whether or not bids are shown, you don't want to be the bottom of the bucket. Sometimes you will even get a project because you bid the highest and therefore look like the best. Often, I think clients award the project to a writer with a reasonable bid in the middle that shows expertise in both writing and the subject matter.

Most full length ghostwriting projects go for $3000 to $5000. The low end would be $2500. Some nice projects go for $5000 to $10,000 for writers with experience, great reviews and successful projects that show their writing will sell. Having novels that sell has helped me get good fees for my ghostwriting projects.

Ebooks, which are usually much shorter, can be quick, easy projects where you write 20 to 50 pages for $200 to $500. Longer ebooks can pay $300 up to $800.

I often start with a $10 per page estimate for writing, but that's after a couple years of experience and reviews to back it up.

For editing, you can charge something like 1 to 2 cents per word, or a per page fee, like .85 cents. If you charge by the page for writing, editing or critiquing, always define what a page is.

I define pages either by manuscript format: 8.5 by 11, double spaced, 1 inch margins,

Or print format: 5x8, single spaced, .5 inch margins.

Resources for Pricing:

I really like this post because it talks about factoring in the value you bring.
http://www.copyblogger.com/pricing-freelance-writing/

This article is about charging per hour or a flat rate:
http://freelancewrite.about.com/od/finances/f/rates.htm

I do not like to charge by the hour, which is a personal preference. I feel that I'm a very fast worker, but I offer high value. I also don't want to keep track of hours, so it's much easier for me to charge per page or calculate a fee for a page range such as 150 – 175. However, I've noticed many other people want to charge per hour to ensure they're fairly compensated.

This article offers advice and a list of what to charge for different kinds of projects:
http://www.freelancewriting.com/articles/how-to-set-your-freelance-writing-rates.php
It does set the fees a bit higher than I've seen on a freelancer site. Maybe you can bid high and win jobs, and if so, go for it!

I'm providing these links as additional resources on top of my advice. In case you're wondering, I give just a short summary because I don't want to take away from other writers. They offer some good information and advice.

Sites and Resources

Here's a list of sites I've used and more resources from online:

www.guru.com

www.elance.com

www.ifreelance.com

www.demandstudios.com

The Top 10 Freelancing Sites. I really like this list and the info it gives. Yes, they list Guru and Elance. http://pcandweb.com/resources/top-10-freelance-sites-why-start-freelancing.html

10 Best Sites to Start Your Freelancing Career:
http://emoneymakingonline.com/2010/07/02/10-sites-start-freelancing-career/

The Monster List of Freelancing Sites:
http://freelanceswitch.com/finding/the-monster-list-of-freelancing-job-sites/

I've included these extra lists in case you get ambitious and want to bid on a variety of sites. You can notice from my story that I used three, and usually two of them at time.
I'd like to point out what I think makes a good freelancing site:

Is the site easy to use and navigate?

Does the site have you create a work agreement? There should be some kind of formal statement detailing the job uploaded to the site. This keeps you and the client on the same page, and helps everyone agree when the work is completed.

Does the site have escrow? This means, once you agree upon a free with a client, you are able to bill them and have the money stored through the freelance site.

Does the site have arbitration? If you run into problems, and have payment in escrow, many sites will step in and help work things out.

More Resources:

Reliable Writers. 73 resources for online freelance writers. This page has sections full of links on how to improve your writing, establishing a writing business, where to find jobs, writing for the web, and links about software. http://www.reliablewriters.com/blog/2009/10/73-resources-for-online-freelance-writers/

This Freelance Folder has all kinds of tools to improve your writing and help with freelancing. It's more focused on downloads and software than links and articles. http://freelancefolder.com/fifty-free-resources-for-freelance-writers-bloggers-and-others/

Notes:

Red Flags

This is where I can really save you some headaches. The biggest red flag is when anyone is abusive or demeaning. I've only seen this a few times, but there's a chance you might run into someone who will put you down, be rude or insulting, or somehow make it very difficult to work with them. If you consider their behavior wrong, it's just not worth it. Even if you've started work on a project, you can walk away. It's better to lose a little income than end up with a huge headache. I feel I need to provide that warning, so I should also say I've only ran into completely unacceptable behavior twice.

There are many other, much smaller, red flags. I've developed this list based on my experience. I noticed patterns and realized whenever I saw these statements and bid or accepted a job, there were always problems later on.

Whenever I see any of these in a project description, I run:

- This is an easy job for a good writer, so bid low.

- I have a ton of projects so bid fairly.

- This is the first of many projects, and I'll pay more next time.

- I'm looking for cheap…. (anything)

- Any demands for low bids, such as "250 articles for $50."

Why are these bad? These buyers will continue to beat up you on price. They'll talk you down, and then they often try to get a discount after everything is agreed to. They'll demand numerous rewrites and edits, and then say that you have to give them a discount for this, such as dropping the final milestone. It's funny, but these people demand a rock bottom price but they are never happy with the product, even after they overwork you.

There's some flawed logic in the promise of continued work too. Why should you give them a fee that's below fair just because they have more jobs for you? Two bucks an hour, forever, yippee! No, thank you. Save yourself and skip bidding on these.

In fact, whenever a new buyer has talked me down on my fee, something went wrong in the project. I've had cases where people posted a high project budget and then talked me down to a fee lower than the budget. Just as an example, the posted budget would be something like $1000- $3000 and I would bid $1500. Then the buyer would want me to lower the price as low as $700. They baited me with a high budget, and that's just not right.

I've noticed that when people accept my bid and my fee without negotiating, they're usually happy throughout the project and give me a great review. When, on the other hand, they beat me up on price, things always get weird. They would walk away after a milestone but before the project's completion. Or they demanded extra work.

I know negotiating is a normal part of life and many jobs, but this pattern has been clear and consistent for me.

Run whenever a client asks for a free work sample. Most sites prohibit this and will delete a posted project that demands every bidder complete a task for free. You have work samples, so you don't need to write 10 pages, a chapter or edit a chapter for free. I have edited a page of a few paragraphs to show someone my style with their writing, but that's as far as I'll go.

Why is this bad? Well, if this was allowed, you would be writing all kinds of free work. I saw this quite a bit when I first started, before most of the sites prohibited it, and I didn't see it turn into work.

Watch out for vague project descriptions. If the buyer isn't sure what they want, it's hard to create pay points or to conclude the job. It's also harder to show you've finished the work. The buyer is more likely to feel that you didn't fulfill expectations too.

The Sneaky Red Flag

If the project is based on existing material, you should be able to see a sample before accepting a project award, and ideally before making a bid.

For editing projects, there should be a sample chapter.

For rewriting projects, there should be a sample article.

And if a client emails or calls to discuss a project, you should always ask to see either the full manuscript that you would be editing or their material for anything you will ghostwrite.

Why can this be a red flag? I once accepted a 50 page editing project based on text that had been pasted into an email. When I received the file of 50 pages, it was in 8 point font, single spaced, and had no margins. It was actually 100 or more pages of writing.

Other times I've accepted editing projects based on a small sample, but the rest of the work needed much more editing.

So be careful if the client doesn't want to show you the work involved. It's okay if they ask you to sign a nondisclosure agreement, or NDA before sending work. Just read it over and make sure it's not more than an agreement to keep the material confidential.

All of these warnings might boil down into this: only work with people who treat you as a professional.

You know that saying, a lawyer is worth her weight in gold? When you really need a good lawyer, you don't negotiate their fee. If you need a good surgeon, you go the best, not the cheapest. Be the best at what you do, and expect fair compensation.

There can be red flags after you begin work on a project too. Beware of anyone who asks you to submit work before they pay the down payment or deposit money into escrow. I've had one client take the work and run, and that was enough for me to require a down payment or escrow. Even if the down payment is $50 or $100, it gets them to make a commitment and show they are professional. I've found that when you write a small down payment into the work agreement, 90% of clients accept it. They understand that this is your job, and you don't have any guarantee that they're an upstanding person.

The other red flag I've ran into is clients who change the project after we've started. Normally, it wasn't a change to the workload but something about the theme or tone of the material itself. One person wanted to take a memoir in a different direction that I wasn't comfortable writing. Another person hired me based on the introduction for the book we would write together. Later, they weren't happy with it at all. It seemed this client didn't know what they wanted, and so I couldn't provide it. The way to protect yourself here is to include a down payment and clear milestones. Also include a clause in your work agreement that you don't provide refunds. If you write 50 pages and they decide to cancel the project at 75, for whatever reason, they should not be able to demand a refund of the 50 page pay point. That paid for your time and services.

Of course you should work with clients, and provide edits, but sometimes you'll run into people that are never happy with things.

It's very different if someone pays for work that you can't complete. That's another reason to break your fee down into pay points. That way, you get paid for the points you reach. If either of you needs to cancel a project, the rest of the pay points are cancelled as well.

There are probably different views and ideas on this, and I'm just providing information on the way I do it.

Managing Your Work Load

Once you begin winning jobs, the issue of managing your projects and time arises. The first consideration is when you'll work. Some people need a structured work day or time during the day. Others might be working on freelance work after their day job, classes or at night. You can choose and create this, which is the fun part and can also be the hard part.

I work while my kids are in school and sometimes when they're off school but busy. I began ghostwriting when my youngest child had a half day, four days a week. That was less work time. Now all my children go to school four days a week, but the days are longer than the normal five day week.

My workday includes time for exercise and running errands if needed, and usually a few chores around the house. Some days I might spend most of the time writing and other times I might take the entire day off. I've always used my time for both "work" projects and my own writing. These days, I spend most of my time on my writing.

The biggest advice I can give here is to take yourself and your work seriously. Other people might think that because you're working at home, you're not really working. They might want to stop in and don't understand that, while you're working, they're showing up at your workplace. Even if you're just bidding, you're working. So if you need to, go ahead and tell people you're working and can't visit.

Imagine that you have a deadline and out-of-town family or friends decide to drop by for the day or even several days. It's just too stressful! So you have to be firm about your work time.

This can even apply to yourself. I love the freedom of working from home, but sometimes I know I really cut into my productive time by playing around online. My phone is next to me and beeps when I get an email. I also find myself spending time on Facebook, Twitter and reading articles. Some of this is okay. I think our minds need a break, and much of my online time is related to book promoting. But I have to watch myself if I have a challenging project and it's dragging out. That usually means I'm taking breaks every twenty minutes.

You don't have to feel bad at all if you take a break, do something else or even go have some fun. It's all about getting the work done before the agreed date, and you get to manage that.

I hope everything goes smoothly for you, but if you feel something is off, it might help to write down your hours and some notes to see where your time is going.

If you aren't finding work, review your online presence. Recheck your website and freelancer profiles for errors. Is everything upbeat and positive? Do you have work samples? Take a look at other freelancer profiles, especially top earners or freelancers who won projects you bid on. You won't always find the answers in their profile, but you might see things they're doing that you're not.

If you're not paying for the highest level membership, upgrade. I've found I get the most work by being a "vender" or whatever they call they're more expensive memberships.

With your higher membership level, you should have some perks to use. Spend more points on the premium bids. This makes a huge different.

When I bid these days, I only bid on a project I will really enjoy, and I make a premium bid. That puts me up at the very top of the list of bidders, and the site usually marks me as the #1 recommended freelancer or in the top three.

Now look at your bids to ensure they're positive, upbeat and detailed.

Beyond that, you might need to bid more often on more projects, and on more sites. I think a normal win rate is around 10%.

There will also be slower periods where you don't win as many projects or don't see many you want. When that happens, I hit all the sites hard. If one isn't working, another might.

I've had times where things were really slow and then I won six projects all at once. Then several people would call about publishing. The lesson there is to put away some money when you're earning extra.

Managing your Work Projects

For the first year or two, I created and printed out a "job board" to hang in my work area. It was a simple chart where I could list my jobs and fill in updates so I knew where the project was. You can easily do this on a white board, on paper or even in a notebook.

Somewhere along the line, I switched this to my computer and began using a little program called Sticky Notes. I might have a note listing my project and its progress:

Waiting on down payment
Write first chapter before 10-24
Waiting on feedback for ch. 10
Sent to employer, complete, waiting on pay

For most of my freelance/ghostwriting time, I've had one or two big projects. These full length book projects for me. I also tried to have some ebooks, articles or editing for smaller jobs. Sometimes, on top of this, I had one to three publishing packages.

The trick is to keep a full workload without getting overwhelmed. When you have work, keep bidding. It can take a few days, a few weeks, or even a few months for some jobs to move from bidding and talking to awarding. I've had people come back a year or two later with a project we discussed. So if you have a full workload, don't stop bidding. I've done that a few times and then ended up with a dead spell.

You'll have to figure out where your "overwhelmed" point is. When I found myself feeling like I had way too much to get done, I would figure out which project had the closest pay point. Oh, I can finish this chapter and send it to the client. So I would work on that project, focus on it and not stress about the others. Once that was sent off, I'd go to the next project with the closest pay point. At first, I worried someone might discover I had to work on another project before theirs, but I have never once had anyone upset with me and asking where the material was.

If you do reach a point where you're behind and running into problems, talk to the client. Let me know if some circumstance came up that will delay you. Even if you've taken on more than you can handle, it's till appropriate to communicate this somehow.

I've experienced this on the buyer end, and I'll share the story to illustrate how it can negatively affect a client, the project and possibly your future projects as a freelancer. I've posted a few projects and hired freelancers to help me with my books. Once I needed a proof reader for *Book Promoting 101.* I marked about ten freelancers as favorites out of all the bidders and awarded the job to a woman about my age. She was excited and began right away. Within a week, I received the first few pages with all kinds of notes, comments and heavy editing. She had even changed the wording in the table of contents, which was automatically created from my chapter names. I wrote back and explained that I only needed proof reading, and maybe a light edit if she felt it was needed. This project didn't have a big budget and I didn't expect the freelancer to do much more than proof read.

I realized she was performing a full critique, edit and proof reading, which should be three separate steps. So I told her that perhaps she had mixed this project up with a different project. I nicely explained that she didn't need to do so much. After this, I expected that she would switch to simply proof reading, which would be much less work, and it was what we agreed upon.

I always listen carefully to my clients and adjust my editing or writing style, or even what I'm doing if they decide they need something else. (We sometimes change the project agreement and fee if we both agree to adjusting a project.) In this case, I simply wanted what we agreed to and what I planned to pay for.

At this point, she became very angry and told me she could not continue with the project if I "simply couldn't put a sentence together."

I was baffled, to say the least. This book had undergone serious review with five other authors. After some thought, I concluded that she was either undergoing some emotion strain, had either mixed up the jobs and became embarrassed, or was overwhelmed with too many projects or life in general.

Now, I'm the kind of person that likes to get things done yesterday. I wanted to get the book out, and I had just spent two weeks on this freelancer. One of the original bidders that I also liked lived in Eugene, under two hours away from me. I liked Wendell Anderson's credentials and professional manner, and I hired him. He did a wonderful job of light editing and proof reading, and I thanked him in the front of the book.

In this case, I encountered problems at the beginning of the project and it only cost me two weeks of time. There wasn't money in escrow or a down payment, and the freelancer walked away after those first few pages. Imagine, however, if there was money involved or she had worked on several chapters. We might have ended up in arbitration through the site about whether I needed to pay her anything.

Freelancing sites allow both clients and freelancers to leave reviews for the other. Many sites do this after each paid invoice at a pay point, so you can receive several reviews on a larger project. If the above project had gone past a pay point, I could have left a poor review for the freelancer. See how getting overwhelmed can hurt your future projects?

Because we didn't reach a pay point, I emailed the site and let them know about the situation. That's something I might sometimes just to document a situation. I learned that this site, and probably other sites, keep complaints on record and will review a freelancer if they receive too many. That, too, can hurt your future earning ability.

This story could have been completely different if the freelancer communicated with me in a constructive way. If you have no choice but to step down from a project, with a professional explanation, your client might be disappointed but most people understand life happens.

I had someone hire me for quite a bit of ongoing work. But then she disappeared, leaving the last invoice unpaid. I emailed several times and sent an invoice reminder, and finally decided I wasn't going to hear from her again. The money involved was under $100 and I really didn't think she would purposely skip out on it. Something probably happened. It was a good six months later when I got an email from her explaining that her engagement fell through and that she had been dealing with a lot of things. She felt horrible when she went through her email and realized she hadn't paid me, so she sent payment with a bonus.

Life happens on both ends, and honest communication is the always the best option.

Managing the Financial Side

I already mentioned that it's a good idea to put money away when you can. Freelancing means your income goes up and down. In the best situation, it will go up and down but stay above your baseline, or the amount of money you need to keep going.

To determine your baseline, write out all your expenses from fixed payments to gas, food, clothing, etc. I know, we're talking about a budget, but if you don't like budgets just call it something else like "My Money Plan."

Just like I enjoy choosing my work, I like to pick what's important to me. I make those things happen. There are lots of things that I don't personally need. When you're self employed, you can control your baseline more than someone with a commute, who needs work clothes and might have other job related expenses. If you haven't checked all the frugal living sites online, you'll be amazed if you take some time and google it.

I've been able to live the way I want on a smaller budget than others. We live on the river so we can save money by staying home and enjoying the outdoors. We've traveled internationally and on trips around Oregon, but we know how to adjust things if less money comes in on a given month.

Of course, one answer to money issues is to earn more. The beauty about this kind of work is you can find more sites, bid on more projects, bid higher, expand your services, or even do other kinds of odd jobs because you're not tied to a contract or company. I like to call it "giving myself a raise." As I gained experience, I bid higher. If I have several projects, I'll bid high. I also write and publish my own books, so a new book is another revenue stream.

Another smart move? Don't bid on low paying jobs. You'll waste your time and might be too busy to take higher paying jobs. I get invited to projects all the time. I used to bid on most of them but these days, I only bid on a few. The reason is many have very low budgets. If you want "quick cash," bid on a bunch of small projects such as articles, ebooks, web content or research papers.

There is a big different between small, easy projects and low paying projects. "Low paying" means it involves a lot of work for a little money, like editing 500 pages for $250 or writing 150 pages for $50. Sometimes a project will look like good pay until you do the math, so it's a good idea to check.

There are articles and ebook projects that pay pretty well for 20 to 50 pages of writing. When you search for projects, set the minimum budget setting for $250 to weed out those low paying ones. Value your time and expertise.

Finding Local Work

I haven't talk about finding work locally yet, and that's because I find the bulk of my work online. However, word of mouth spreads. After I launched my self publishing company, I had local people call me because they heard about me from the community. Some work came through my local writing group too. Most of this work was publishing with a few editing, critiquing and writing jobs.

If you're starting a company or a full time career, you might want to consider the local market. You can reach people through writing and publishing events, and by getting to know the writing groups and book store owners in the area. We have quite a few of these in Oregon, including some big events in Portland. I think, however, a lot of local work comes in a roundabout way. Let me explain.

I held a small launch party for *Book Promoting 101* in my local town of Roseburg, Oregon in early 2011. I wrote the book for my publishing clients, and I held the event because I thought it'd be fun. I arrived to find several people waiting and more came in as we got started. It was a book signing, but much more. We spent several hours discussing writing, publishing and promoting, and had a great time.

A lady named Anna Willman came and we discussed her work in progress, a 600 page local history of the Confidence Clinic in Roseburg, Or. She planned to donate the book proceeds to the clinic.

Several writing friends came by, including an author friend of mine came by named B.K. Mayo. I have several guest articles in *Book Promoting 101*, and he had wrote one about fundraising with books. (He had donated proceeds from his book, *Tamara's Child*, to a teen pregnancy center.)

These two began talking and hit on this connection, and that convinced her to buy *Book Promoting 101*. It was about six months later when she called me because she was ready to publish the book.

While I was working on this publishing package, I was invited to an event in Eugene, about an hour north of me, that would highlight different book services. They invited two illustrators, two editors, two publishers, and so on. I attended as a self publisher and writing service provider, and I also took copies of *Book Promoting 101* to sell.

I made some great connections at the event and sold quite a few books. While I was there, the president of the local writing group that hosted the event came by to talk to me. It turned out she was Anna's daughter in law, and that's why I got the call to come.

It's amazing how all these little connections start coming together. You can create them by carrying business cards and telling people what you do. Join events in your area, either as service provider or an author if you are one. This is one more way to find freelancing work, and it can be very rewarding when you get to work with people face to face.

This wraps up the information about strictly freelancing. The next section offers tips and advice on how to grow your reader base as a novelist or nonfiction writer.

Notes:

Co-Writing and Your Writing

This is the section for freelance writers who are also developing a career in writing their own books.

Co-writing might come up if you bid on creative projects. I've co-written two novels now where the client had created the characters and plot line but found they weren't able (or didn't have time) to fill in the story. Clients will be more open to co-writing if you have published works that are selling. Of course, it might not be an option you want to pursue.

Consider if co-writing will help market the book more. Will be benefit both you and the client? Is the book something you want your name associated with?

If someone comes to you (a working freelance writer) with a co-writing project, it should still be a paid project. I recommend getting a down payment, pay points, and a percentage of the royalties.

I do know of authors who team up and co-write a book together, either with both names or a single pen name. That's a different situation than what I'm talking about, and one that I haven't personally tried yet. My experience lies in clients coming to me with a book idea. It might be you don't encounter any co-writing opportunities while working on freelancing sites. If you do, you'll need to consider the terms, the work involved and if it's a good opportunity for you.

I loved co-writing because I enjoyed filling out the plot, and it was fun to have that collaborative energy. It was also a chance to be paid to write fiction in both cases.

Now let's talk about your writing. You might be writing novels or nonfiction books, or maybe both. Both take good writing and marketing. Nonfiction needs a platform. Readers want to know why you're an expert and how you can help them. If you write well, and can offer a great solution, it'll be much easier to find readers. One of the easiest ways to reach readers and let them know you have useful information is to blog about it. Instead of launching a big sales site, offer information. People will trust you more and see that you know what you're talking about. If you offer some good information, people will buy the book for more.

Fiction needs a readership, which means a group of people who become fans and look forward to your next book.

My advice for fiction writing is to keep writing and keep publishing.

The simple way to improve your writing is to read, write and repeat. The more you read, write and practice, the better you'll get.

The beauty in that is the more books you write, the better your storytelling and writing will be. And having more books means more income streams.

Donald Maass, one of the most known literary agents, said it takes about 5 books for things to take off. (Check out The Breakout Novelist and his other books on writing and publishing. Very good stuff.)

Of course a few writers have had their first book go big, but the pattern with most authors is that they have quite a few books out there before their sales start climbing.

I've seen this in other writers, and my sales took off after five books. So while everyone wants the shortcut, the real way is to just keep writing. If you love writing, this isn't bad news either.

There are hundreds of books on writing out there, so I won't try to cover good writing in this little book. The most important novel writing advice is to have a big enough conflict – tell a good story! This should be an inner struggle that is also represented through the physical world. Look up everything by Donald Maass, books by Writer's Digest, read your favorite authors and get good, professional critiques.

On to promoting then. Just like we have a ton of books about writing, there are all kinds of promoting resources. I published a book called *Book Promoting 101*, which contains several guest articles. I'll include a few of the tips from that book in the following pages. Some of the book applies to offline promoting so I won't include all of that. (That information was more for my publishing clients because many of them weren't sure where to start with book promoting.) If you're interested, you can get the book on Kindle, PDF or in print.

I also run a blog at www.bookpromoting101.com that focuses on online promoting for ebooks. I'll pull a few of the most popular posts right off the blog and include them in this section.

Think of Promotion as a Rolling Snowball

Once you have several books out there, it's time to grow your audience. I use Facebook and Twitter to reach out to readers. Readers love to hear about upcoming books and giveaways. I personally don't think they like hearing about how many words you wrote today or complaining about things that bugged you. People like fun, positive people online.

This might sound like an odd idea, but book promotion is like a rolling snowball. Every little thing you do to promote your book adds to the snowball. But when you drop the ball and forget about promoting your book, it all disappears. It melts.

It's true that you can generate big results if you can promote your book full time, but it's also true that you can do this by devoting an hour a day, or doing one promotion task each day. When you do little and big things here and there to promote your book, it adds up to steady sales.

- Network on Twitter and Facebook, sharing others' good news and retweeting people.
- Guest blog. Book bloggers are always asking authors to guest blog or join a promotion of some kind.
- Donate ebooks to book bloggers for their blog hops, events and giveaways. I like their pages on Facebook and join their conversations. It's not about pushing your book on people, but getting to know them and then joining their events.
- Join blog hops related to your genre.
- Hold your own giveaway or contest.

- Submit your book to book bloggers for review. Read over their websites and follow their submission guidelines.
- Get your book listed or mentioned in a new website, blog, article or physical location.
- Send out a newsletter, email or other communication.
- Run an ad in a paper, Google, Facebook, other publication.
- Launch a new promotion, contest or giveaway.
- Get a reader or professional review.
- Attend a writing conference.
- Speak to a local writer's group, an online group, or a reader group.
- Publish more books.
- Enter a writing contest.
- Enter a book contest.

Marketing experts know people are more likely to buy something they've seen in several places such as on TV, a magazine and the side of a bus. We see images all the time that make an impression. When a reader has heard about your book or your name from different people, different ads, an article and other places, they might look your website or book up online, or they might even find the book in a bookstore. If they've heard about you and then see you at a bookstore, they're much more likely to buy a book.

Every little and big thing you do creates another impression. These add together online, and more links and mentions puts you higher in search engines. Name brands use this to become household names. By promoting your work, you are branding yourself. If you're unsure of what I mean, think of Steven King. Did you think of mushy romances? No, you thought of his horror books that have become movies.

Different authors have different brands:
- Nicholas Sparks writes Southern tragedies with a lyrical writing voice.
- Nora Roberts writes suspenseful romances.
- Agatha Christie wrote mysteries that are still popular.

If you think of yourself and your work as a product you are selling, it's easier to see why you want to promote your writing as much as possible. If you love your writing, it can be fun to talk about it, write about it and connect with readers.

Being an author can be a blast, and many ways to market your book are fun. One of the easiest marketing tips I've ever heard is: Enthusiasm is contagious. Smiling is contagious. Smile and show your enthusiasm when you're talking to people, even on the phone. Did you know other people can tell when you smile over the phone?

Your attitude comes across loud and clear online as well. Being a positive person goes a long way toward building your author brand.

If you feel discouraged while promoting, remember that promotion is like a snowball. You will probably see a rise in sales after events and promotions. Afterwards, sales will drop again. Don't give up! Later, you'll announce something new, and people will remember your earlier promoting and buy a book. Or maybe they'll hear about you for the first time and then see everything you've done. All these will add together to give you traction that keeps sales going. Think about promoting as a business, but one you can have fun with.

Content is King

This is a huge tip for nonfiction writers. If you're trying to sell nonfiction, you need to offer some information on your website.

The internet is an information and content war.

This is useful for anyone who is looking for specific information. Yet, this makes it a bit hard to draw traffic into your site.

The answer is to offer good information on a regular basis. Update your website and blog with information that visitors will want to read. If you advertise your books constantly, just trying to make a sale, you will make less sales!

The websites and blogs with the most useful information get the most online traffic. You want to offer more than just a sales pitch for your book. Give people a reason to come to your website or blog, and give them reasons to return.

Google all your favorite authors and look over their websites and blogs. Often you'll find an interesting bio, writing tips, resources for writers, tour dates, links, blogs about getting an agent, the publishing process, what the writer is dealing with during revisions and reviews.

I came across many very useful blogs and websites whiles researching promoting, and one in particular called The Creative Penn (www.thecreativepenn.com) ran by Joanna Penn. It offers monthly ezines, a constant supply of articles on writing, publishing and promoting, and the blogger is very active on her blog. If you comment, she'll often comment back the same day. It's a giant information hub for authors. I bookmarked it on my computer, "liked" her Facebook page, and plan to read her new articles.

Joanna Penn is also a fiction writer. She just released her second book this month, January 2012. Her online presence appears to be a huge help to her book promotion.

People love to learn, and the Internet makes it possible to "goggle" any subject for instant learning. If you don't offer new and useful information, along with your books, you'll lose readers to better sites.

Offering great information is the way to find new readers and turn them into customers.

How To Promote Ebooks

You can promote an ebook in many of the same ways you would a print version, but you also have extra marketing avenues. It's so easy for someone to see a book that looks interesting, click the ad or link and go to the Amazon page, and purchase your book with one click. You can purchase ads like this on Facebook, Google Adwords, LinkedIn, Goodreads and other sites. Some authors find they get a good return on paid promotions.

I've found free promotions work the best for me. It's putting in time and energy instead of money. These include spending time blogging, guest blogging, submitting to book review blogs, interacting with book bloggers and readers online, and offering free chapters or entire books. Readers love giveaways and prizes too.

Kindle, Nook and iBook readers are looking for great books and good deals, and they sign up for all kinds of lists and websites to get this information sent to them. Just take a look at Kindle Nation Daily and all the ways you can sponsor them for wide exposure.

World Library (Facebook page) lists bargain and free Kindle books. The owner will also feature your book on his blog. Search Facebook for book pages and you'll find book review pages, genre specific pages, bargain books and many more people who love to read and talk about it. Some pages are for bargain and free ebooks while others focus on a type of reader such as Kindle or Nook.

Other ways to promote a Kindle book: visit your book's Kindle page on Amazon and fill in tags, or words people will use to search for books. Add a link to the Kindle version (and other versions) to your blog, website, email signature and any articles you publish, if possible.

Seven Secrets to Selling eBooks

I have a new secret to share, even though it might make some people groan:

Time.

It takes time, just like anything worth wanting. I know we keep seeing outrageously huge success stories about a book suddenly shooting up the charts and making thousands or even millions, but I also know there's a lot of time and effort behind that. I don't think most books that sell well are published and shoot up the charts. They might for known authors or authors with a really effective marketing plan with unique aspects, but I think if you're reading this, you're looking for a way to sell more ebooks. I personally think about reaching more readers because my goal is to build a reader base for a long term writing career.

So how do you best leverage time? You just keep at it. I look for and figure out new things to do to get my name and books out, and try to do something every few days, whether it's big or small. I study authors that are highly successful and adopt and adapt their methods.

One thing you'll notice through the following tips is that I keep on top of what's going on and take advantage of everything I can.

Here's a few things I've done this year: (2011)

1. As stated, I put some thought and time into promoting. I try to work smarter, not harder, by setting clear goals and measuring results. I read all the popular books like *The Career Novelist* by

Donald Maass, John Locke's book *How I Sold 5 million ebooks,* and a bunch of blogs about writing and promoting. My promoting time is often spent connecting with readers and reaching more readers, while trying not to be a continuous promoter. I run from those kind of authors myself! My promoting time is often promoting someone else, helping someone else, writing a fun post or sharing fun things about my life.

2. I priced my Kindle books at 99 cents (like Amanda Hocking.) I previously blogged that $2.99 is better, but then when I ran my books at a 99 cents special, they started really selling. Since my goal is to gain readers, I kept my books at 99 cents and used that as a promotion tool. I have a page on Facebook to advertise mine, and any other 99 cent romances, at www.facebook.com/99CentRomances. So come like it and post your 99 cent romances! This is another way I try to help other authors and readers. On a side note, this one is a personal choice since you get a much bigger percentage of the book royalty at $2.99 and above. If you want to make more money per book or only have one book, you might want to try a different tactic.

3. I switched my website to a blog because search engines like them better and they're more interactive. Yes, my hits went up, and now I can blog on my website. (Joe Konrath and Amanda Hocking both use blogs, and even the free version.)

4. I've been submitting books to book review blogs, and even blogs that just list or feature books, all through the year. I find them mostly on Facebook and network with them instead of just cold-sending my books to people who don't know me from Jo or

Jane. I think most authors are submitting to book bloggers, so the wait is getting longer and longer. That's why it takes time. But once you get several reviews out there on those blogs, and hopefully posted to Amazon and Goodreads, your sales go up. (As long as it's a good review, I suppose. 4 or 5 stars.)

5. I joined Twitter this year. I know, I was late on that one! I checked it out before and didn't like the way it's set up for marketing, but everyone is on there. So I joined and I follow people I find interesting. I don't autofollow, which tics some people off, but I also don't want anyone to follow me just for a follow back. I want to interact with people I find interesting, and I want people to follow me because they want to read my tweets. I have met some great people, and I made the process easier for me by linking my author Facebook page. Now my FB posts go on Twitter too, and then I can go and retweet people and enjoy it more. Has it helped? I think more people see my book stuff. I try to be fun and not too "promoty" on FB and Twitter, so I think readers might find my interesting and fun and check out my books – they're listed in my bio. *Since writing this blog, I've been using free books more and more, and Twitter is a great way to get the word out about great deals and freebies. People aren't on there to buy books, so I think it's best to keep your promoting to free books and celebrating big milestones.

6. Giveaways have worked miracles for me, but I'll admit it doesn't appear to help everyone. I think if you have a great book that you give away for a while, that will attract readers. I discovered this in

the summer of 2011. When I gave away a book, that book's sales would rise along with all my other ebooks.

In December of 2011, I gave away 45,000 ebooks and sold 9,000. It was my best sales month to date.

7. So here's my biggest lesson from this year, from watching other authors and my own results. Readers run from authors who seem angry that people aren't buying their books, or upset about restrictions that self published authors face, or even bitter about the public not embracing every single author that pens a book. Readers love authors who have spent the time and money to have an attractive, professional cover and book, and know how to politely and positivity represent themselves online. In short, readers enjoy interacting with authors that are happy to be published and feel blessed to have this awesome opportunity to put a book out into the world and share it. You have to earn readers. Writing a book does not earn readers. Writing the best book you can, and being a good friend to others, earns you readers.

Of course, there's lot of other little tricks and tactics that help authors to different degrees, such as Amazon tags on your book page, networking, groups and many more. These are 7 bigger things that have helped me. I hope they help you too!

What's Next?

I sincerely hope you've found many useful ideas for becoming a full time writer in this book. I invite you to take my ideas and tweak, evolve and alter them. Find what works for you. This is especially true when it comes to your writing and how you promote your books.

Visit   www.bookpromoting101.com   for more promoting ideas or to share your own. I welcome comments on this book and how things are going for you as a writer.

If you're an author as well as freelancer, you might want to check out *Book Promoting 101* and *How To Sell More Kindle eBooks*.

The best of luck to you!

Kristen James

About The Author

Kristen James loves to watch wildlife in her yard and on the river by her house. Besides reading and writing, she loves traveling, cycling, hiking, berry picking, canoeing, fishing and camping, and especially doing these with her family. Life should be an adventure!

Visit www.writerkristenjames.com to learn more and read her blog.

Connect on Facebook at www.facebook.com/WriterKristenJames

and Twitter at @writerkristenj. She loves to hearing from readers!

Amazon author page with full book list available at http://amazon.com/author/kristenjames